JULIA FOSTER'S PRESENTS

JULIA FOSTER'S PRESENTS

Photographs by Christopher Cormack

Illustrations by Penny Dann

ELM TREE BOOKS · LONDON

Liberty Presents

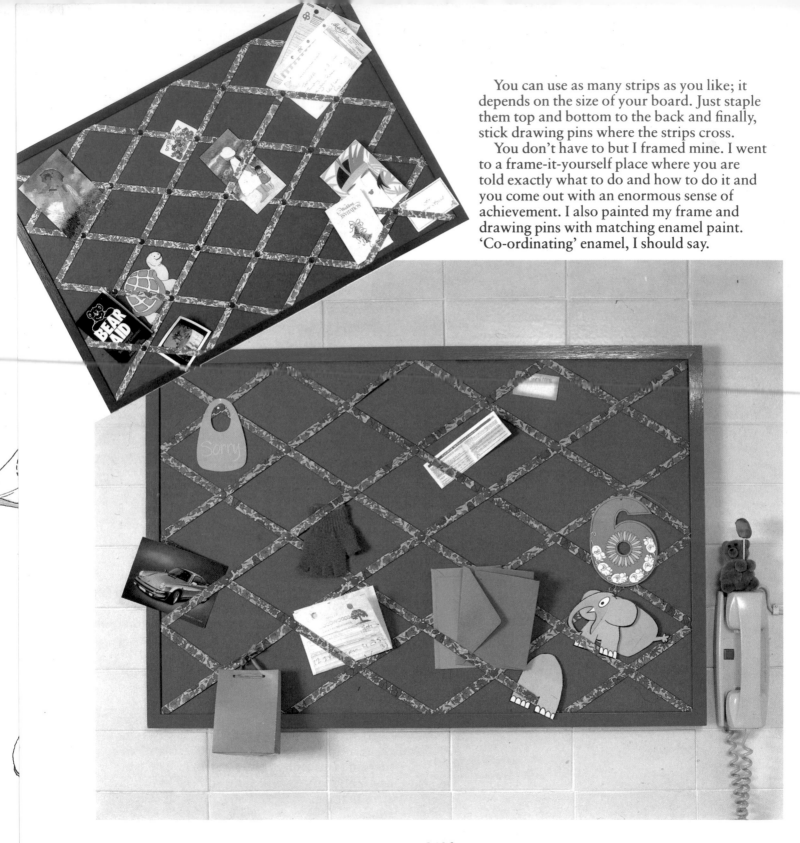

You can use as many strips as you like; it depends on the size of your board. Just staple them top and bottom to the back and finally, stick drawing pins where the strips cross.

You don't have to but I framed mine. I went to a frame-it-yourself place where you are told exactly what to do and how to do it and you come out with an enormous sense of achievement. I also painted my frame and drawing pins with matching enamel paint. 'Co-ordinating' enamel, I should say.

Plaited Mats

I've always wanted to plait. Emily had hair the colour of sunshine when she was three or four and her plaits reached her shoulder-blades. Tamara's hair at the same age was more like very dark chestnuts. She never liked plaits very much – she thought they were rather fancy – and preferred her hair tied back in a ponytail. I even found a chance to plait my own hair. I played a maid in a French farce by Camoletti. Her name was Bridget and I decided she should have red hair (I've always envied Jane Asher's hair). I plaited it and had the plaits over the top of my head. Tom Merrifield did a sculpture of me at the time and I think the plaits look lovely, although most people only notice the corset I was wearing.

The moment I saw a plaited rag rug in America I couldn't wait to make one (see page 45). I've plaited ribbons to make hair bands, I've plaited wool to make belts, so you can imagine how much I was looking forward to plaiting pieces of Liberty print fabric. The result was surprising – not what I was expecting at all, which is why I made some more mats in another colour to see if it made any difference. It didn't. The patterns are so busy that once the plait is ironed flat it hardly looks plaited at all. But I like the result and enjoy making them. A set of six makes a really lovely present.

You will need:
   Three Liberty print fabrics
   Iron-on cotton
   Interfacing
   Medium weight wadding

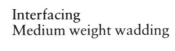

Cut the Liberty print fabric into strips 4cm (1½in) wide and sew several of these together lengthwise. (The number you join together depends on the size of your mat.)

Iron each side under leaving the strips 1.5cm (½in) wide. Hold three pieces together with a pin and plait them together.

Pin one end of the plait into the middle of an ironing board and wind the plait round and round. You can use a few straight pins if you need, to hold everything in place. When you have reached the size you want, tuck the end under.

Iron it all flat taking the pins out as you go.

Now, cut a circle of iron-on fusable cotton either:
   28cm (11in) in diameter for a large mat
   22cm (9in) for a medium mat
   15cm (6in) for a small mat
Place this piece of material on the ironing board with the shiny fusable side up and put your plaited mat on top of it.

As the plaited fabric is not stitched at all you will probably have to rewind it so that it will fit neatly on to the fusable cotton, although once the plait has been ironed flat it is very manageable.

Once the plaited fabric fits perfectly over the fusable cotton, put a piece of fabric over the mat to protect it and iron with a fairly hot iron. If it seems necessary you can stitch the plaits here and there to keep them flat. I stitched some but not others.

Finally, cut a circle of wadding exactly the same size as the fusable cotton and a circle from one of the Liberty fabrics you used in the plait. The fabric circle should be 2cm (¾in) wider all around than the wadding.

Iron the edge of the fabric up over the wadding using a very cool iron (or you'll melt the wadding. I've done *that* before.) Put the plaited fabric face down with the back of the fusable cotton facing you. Lay the backing on top, wadding down, fabric up. Then sew them all together using a matching cotton and tiny stitches.

Picnic Set

I love picnics. Food in the open air always tastes terrific. Actually, food eaten anywhere you are not supposed to eat it tastes good.

My elder daughter Emily was a dreadful eater when she was little. She would eat nothing (although now that she is eighteen she eats everything!). I used to get really desperate about it and one day I set up a tiny table in her plastic Wendy house and sat several teddy bears around it. 'This lot needs feeding,' I said to my rather grumpy three-year-old. Ham sandwiches, nuts, little cups of milk, apples and cut up bananas disappeared into the Wendy house never to be seen again. It was marvellous. She ate everything.

Over the next year Emily ate in the dog's basket, the rabbit hutch, under the bed and in the bath. She fortunately became a better eater as I ran out of strange places in which to feed her! She still enjoys eating on the floor.

I made two of these presents, gave them to a friend and discovered a problem. She asked me for six more (but four would do). I still haven't made them.

Cut two pieces of Liberty print, one 13cm (5in) by 10cm (4in) and the other 13cm (5in) by 6.5cm (2½in) and back these with iron-on cotton.

Using a close together zig-zag stitch on your sewing machine, sew around the edges of both pieces.

Cut a piece of Liberty print 41cm (16in) by 30.5cm (12in). Now place the two previously prepared pieces on to this larger piece as shown below and stitch them into place using the same zig-zag stitch.

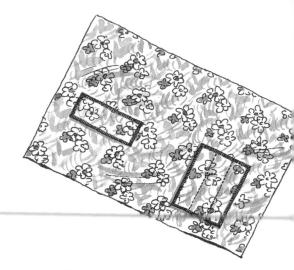

To make the pockets for the cutlery use an ordinary straight stitch.

Now cut strips of Liberty print 7.5cm (3in) wide and join them together until you have a strip about 280cm (110in) in length. Fold this in half lengthways and iron it.

Cut another piece of Liberty print 41cm (16in) by 30.5cm (12in) and a slightly smaller piece of medium weight wadding. Fold the edge of the fabric over the edges of the wadding and tack it into place.

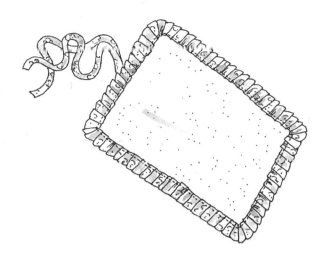

Finally, take the piece of print with the napkin and cutlery holders on it, turn its edges under so that it fits on to the pleated side and stitch it together by hand.

Take the long folded piece of print and pleat it to fit around the edge of the tacked piece of print and wadding. It's easier if you tack the pleats into position as you go.

Make a ribbon (any width you like) out of another piece of Liberty print 112cm (44in) long and tack this into place as you put the pleated fabric round. Once all the fabrics are tacked in place, stitch round with the sewing machine and remove the tacking.

Beaded Mirror

The Chelsea Glass Works in Fulham cut me a round piece of mirror 23cm (9in) in diameter. They also bevelled and polished the edges so they wouldn't be sharp.

I cut a piece of green felt the same size as the mirror and glued it to the back.

Cut a strip of Liberty fabric twice the circumference of the mirror – in my case 142cm (56in) long – and 12.5cm (5in) wide and join the ends to make a circle. Pin a hem under on both sides and iron it.

Using double strand cotton and a tiny running stitch, sew all the way round one of the hems and then gather it up until it fits the mirror and covers about 4cm (1½in) from the edge.

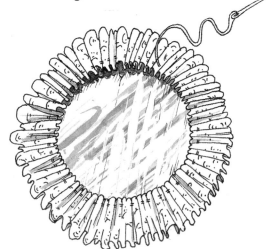

Repeat the same procedure with the fabric on the other side of the mirror.

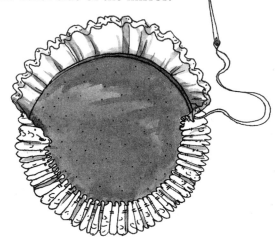

Using double thread once more, sew beads between the gathers on the front of the mirror.

To hang the mirror I made a matching loop and hand stitched it on the back. I wanted a round brass curtain ring but couldn't find one at the time so I used this triangular one. A round one would definitely be better.

Bracelet and Hairband

Cut a strip of Liberty print fabric 61cm (24in) long and 8cm (3in) wide for the hairband, 41cm (16in) long and 8cm (3in) wide for the bracelet. With the right sides together make a 1cm (½in) seam and stitch the entire length of the fabric by machine. Then turn it inside out.

For the headband, take a piece of elastic 30.5cm (12in) long and 2.5cm (1in) wide and thread this elastic into the stitched piece of Liberty print, gathering the material up as you go until it is neatly and evenly ruffled. When you have completed this, stitch the fabric to the elastic at each end. Finally, join the ends with a narrower piece of elastic – for Tamara's head I need 18cm (7in) of this.

Make the bracelet in the same way, but when the elastic is threaded through the fabric sew the ends of elastic together first then turn a small seam under and stitch the fabric around the elastic by hand. I needed 20.5cm (8in) to fit Tamara's wrist.

As Tamara wanted to wear her new striped dress, I rushed back to Liberty's and bought this gorgeous silk taffeta. She'll wear the Liberty print bands another time.

Nightdress Case

I enjoyed making this because it involved dyeing. I find it very satisfying to match something exactly.

This Liberty print was so unusual and the colours so odd that it was fun dyeing the broderie anglaise to match. The satin was easier and I found some that matched perfectly.

Cut a piece of satin, a piece of Liberty print and a piece of medium wadding all the same size – 92cm (36in) by 41cm (16in).

Lay the print face down with the wadding on the top. Put the satin on the wadding face up and tack round the edge. Bind one of the long edges using a piece of satin 8cm (3in) wide and 36cm (14in) long.

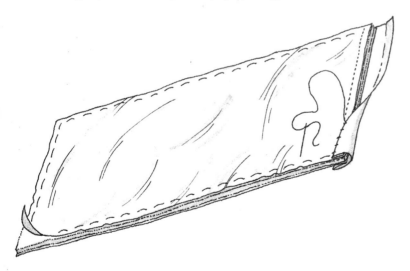

Measure in 30.5cm (12in) from the bound edge, fold this back on itself with the print side outwards and pin it in place. Using your machine, sew the two side seams removing the pins as you go.

You must double sew the seams so that there are no raw edges, so now turn the whole thing inside out and sew the seams again! Then turn it right side out once more.

Cut three pieces of Liberty print 8 cm (3in) wide. Two of them should be 30.5cm (12in) long and one should be 38cm (15in) long. Bind the remaining edges in the same way that you bound the satin edge. You can cut one strip and do it all in one but if you do you will have to mitre the corners, which is fiddly. I found it easier to do the sides separately.

I bought 1 metre (39in) of the kind of broderie anglaise that you thread ribbon through. I washed it (to take the dressing out) and dyed it to match the plum colour in the print.

Cut a one metre (39in) strip of the print 4cm (1½in) wide. Fold the edges under until it's just the right size to thread through the broderie anglaise.

I hand-stitched the threaded broderie anglaise to the front of the case on both sides of the Liberty ribbon. You *must* mitre the corners here. I could find no way to avoid it.

CHILDREN'S

PRESENTS

I enjoy playing with children, little children. My family are into flexing their mental muscles with Scrabble and Trivial Pursuit, but I refuse to play. I'm always beaten. Their minds work faster than mine or they know more trivia and almost everyone in the world spells better than I do. My problem is that when I play I want to win.

That's why I prefer a colouring book, a box of pencils and a pack of Happy Families. I'll play happily for hours with those.

The games I have made are for younger children – and for me! Tamara was quite upset at the thought of giving away the shell game and my son Ben worked out the Solitaire after some weeks of trying, which isn't too bad considering some people never manage to do it at all.

Shell Game

This game is based on the card game Pelmanism. The object is to collect the most pairs.

You will need twenty pairs of shells (although a few extra are a good idea to have as insurance against loss or breakages), and at least twenty pairs of matching stickers.

You could use cockle or mussel shells but I wanted something prettier and found these gorgeous shells in a shop that sells shells, minerals, stones and fossils, just off Charing Cross Road in London.

Clean the shells, keeping them in pairs. Use wire wool and a little diluted bleach if necessary. Once the shells are clean, rinse them and leave them to dry.

Paint the inside of each shell with gold paint. I used 'Dynamic 603 Rich Gold', which you can buy at an artists' supply shop or a DIY centre, and I found I needed two coats to make them a really deep gold.

Once the inside is dry, paint the outside of each shell with a clear high gloss lacquer. I used 'Japlac'. This coat of lacquer protects the shell and keeps the colours bright. It should be left to dry overnight.

Take a pair of matching stickers and a pair of matching shells and stick a sticker on the inside of each shell (on top of the gold paint).

Do the same with the other nineteen pairs of shells. Be sure to use different stickers in each pair, so that you make twenty different pairs.

Using the same clear lacquer, paint the inside of each shell, covering the sticker and the gold paint. That will prevent the stickers getting

picked off. That's it. The shells are ready.

Shells are a little delicate and it's important to find something to keep them in. You could, for example, cover an old cigar box or a chocolate box with material or wrapping paper.

Tamara had been given some writing paper in a very fancy little pink suitcase and told me I could use it for the shells. I divided it with strips of pink cardboard and put some pink cotton wool (and a pair of shells) in each compartment. It all looks quite delightful. I had some stickers left over and put them on the case.

newspaper and leave it to dry. Once the top is dry, turn it over carefully. Allow four or five days total drying time. It takes simply ages to dry.

Once it is dry, sand the edges and any lumps or bumps using fine sandpaper. Once I had done that I painted mine with a high gloss burgundy coloured enamel.

Cut a piece of green felt the size of the finished board and stick it on the bottom. I used an old liqueur chocolates box covered in spotted wrapping paper to 'wrap' it in. I put some green felt in the top and bottom of the box to make it feel a little stronger. Incidentally, don't forget to include the 33 marbles.

Pattern-Making Tiles

I made a game like this many years ago for my 'get well' cupboard.

This cupboard was put together during a whooping cough outbreak. Both my family and my husband's suffer from allergies and so our children were not vaccinated against whooping cough. When the outbreak occurred they all came down with it one by one, in turn. I had one child or another ill in bed for nearly eight consecutive weeks.

The cupboard contains a huge box of postcards which can be sorted into animals, or views, or people, or foreign stamps, or British stamps. There are piles of comics (usually

You can buy tiny tiles used in bathroom mosaic tiling from most DIY shops. They are usually square, although sometimes round or hexagonal, and come in many colours. It's possible to make literally hundreds of different patterns with them.

I made this wooden box to put them in but you can use a shoe box, cigar box or chocolate box. These boxes look wonderful covered with wrapping paper or fabric.

If your child is in bed these tiles work best on a tray placed on the child's lap.

discouraged), sticky paper to cut out, sticker books, boxes of beads, Plasticene, pipe cleaners and multitudes of other things. These tiles provided hours of pattern making.

Dr Who Scarf

I have never really enjoyed knitting. I *can* knit and I *do* knit but I *don't* knit for enjoyment. The last time I knitted anything seriously I was spurred on by a sumptuous sampler pattern Ralph Lauren jumper that cost nearly three hundred pounds. I was driven to prove I could make it for eighteen pounds.

When Ben was about five years old, *Dr Who* was his favourite TV programme and so I decided to make him the scarf. He loved it and even when he grew too old to admit that he ever enjoyed *Dr Who* he still kept the scarf carefully folded in the bottom of his cupboard.

It's really very simple to make. I used Patons wool in nine different colours. With No. 3¾ (9) needles cast on 50 stitches and just knit plain until it is 91cm (7ft) long. The 10cm (4in) fringe was made using different colours of leftover wool.

When Ben saw that I was writing about his scarf I mentioned to him that I was going to say that a Postman Pat scarf might be nice. 'Why not a Triffid scarf?' he asked. 'It could look as though it was strangling the child.' Why *do* children love horrible things?

Oh yes, I must thank our wonderful Katrine for knitting the scarf you see here.

Fishing Rod Case

Cut a piece of waterproof fabric 10cm (4in) wide and 94cm (37in) long, fold it in half lengthways and machine stitch it down its length. This is the strap.

Cut two pieces of fabric 5cm (2in) wide and 40cm (16in) long and stitch the ends of the strap to the middle of each piece.

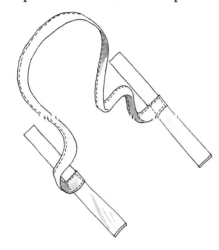

Now cut out the bag. It should be 40cm (16in) wide and 132cm (52in) long. Lay it out and stitch the handle on 46cm (18in) from the bottom and with 46cm (18in) between the two pieces that hold the handle.

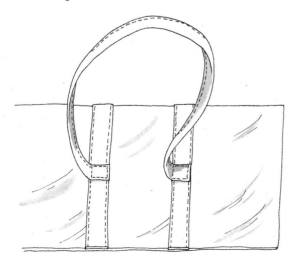

Fold almost in half, leaving one side 1.5cm (½in) longer than the other. Fold this extra 1.5cm (½in) over the shorter side and machine stitch it, leaving 15cm (6in) not stitched at the top.

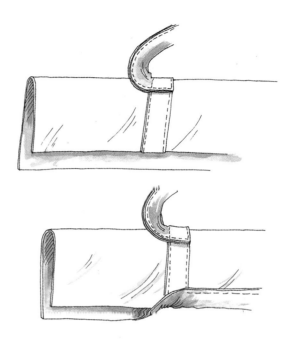

Cut an oval piece of fabric to fit the bottom end of the bag and machine stitch it into place.

I curved the top edge to make it easier to put in a zip. The zip was 36cm (14in) long and heavy duty.

Keepnet Bag

Cut a piece of waterproof fabric 61cm (24in) wide and 91.5cm (36in) long. Turn a 2.5cm (1in) hem in on both 61cm (24in) edges and machine stitch them down. I needed to use a strong needle for this, the one I use for denim.

Fold the right sides together and machine stitch up the sides.

I made two 51cm (20in) handles 10cm (4in) wide, out of the same material. Just fold the strips of material in half lengthways (so they're 5cm/2in wide) and stitch down the edge, then stitch into place on the bag. The finished bag is 46cm (18in) by 56cm (22in) which I'm told will hold a fairly large keepnet.

Heart-Shaped Nightdress Case

Cut out six heart-shaped pieces:

2 Liberty print
2 medium weight wadding
2 lining (I used satin)

The heart should be about 41cm (16in) across and 30.5cm (12in) long.

Place a Liberty print heart right side down, put a piece of wadding on it and lay a lining heart, right side up, on top. Pin the three layers together around the edge.

Using a ruler, draw a line across the middle of the heart at its widest point and carefully cut all three layers in half. Cut two strips of Liberty print 9cm (3½in) wide and bind the edges you have just cut.

Tack round the outside edges of both pieces, removing the pins as you go.

Put the other three heart shapes together in the same way, tack together but do not cut in half.

Make the frill using 15cm (6in) wide pieces of Liberty print. Twice the length of the circumference usually makes a full enough frill but I used three times as I wanted it a bit overdone. I joined the pieces until I had 380cm (150in), folded it in half lengthways and laid a piece of lace edging the same length on it a little lower than the fold. Gather it up using double thread and running stitches.

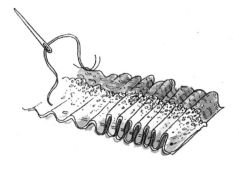

I find it easier to gather half at a time. Divide the long strips of folded print and lace in two, gather one half of the edging to fit into one half of the heart. Repeat with the second half.

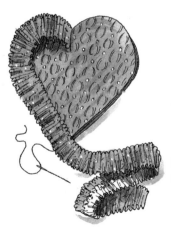

Lay your whole heart out with the Liberty print side facing you. Pin the gathered frill with lace downwards round the edge with the frill facing inwards and tack into place.

Lay the two halves of your other heart on top, right sides together so that the lining is facing you, and tack carefully into place. Where your two halves meet on each side oversew the edges closely together.

Now having checked that everything is in place machine stitch round the edge. Cut the seam back as far as you dare and oversew it using a zig-zag stitch on your machine.

When you turn the case right side out it should be a lovely surprise. Not everything turns out this nice. I added a bow that I was rather pleased with, using leftover lace and a thin (5cm or 2in) strip of Liberty print. After turning in tiny hems on the print, I folded it in half, slipped the plain edge of the lace in between and machine stitched along. I stitched it on the centre point of the heart by hand.

Apple Pyjama Case

Cut two circles of red felt 40.5 cm (16 in) in diameter. From each circle cut a triangle with curved sides, making the two shorter sides 15 cm (6 in) long, like this:

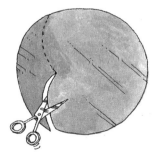

For the lining, cut two pieces of a matching cotton print the same shape as the felt. Cut V shaped notches round the edges, turn these under and iron them flat.

Place the cotton apple shapes right sides together and place a felt shape on each side matching up the shape. Now, using three strands of red embroidery floss sew them all together using a blanket stitch.

To make the opening, when you come to the point where you cut the triangle shape, continue sewing *only one* felt and *one* cotton shape together. Then go back and sew the other side.

Sew a green button on one side at the centre of the triangle and make a green thread loop on the other, to look like the little stem of the apple. It should look good enough to eat!

Tartan Pencil Case

You will need:

70cm (¾yard) tartan material – I used a
lightweight Liberty cotton
70cm (¾yard) lightweight wadding
50cm (20in) red cotton material
24 coloured pencils

Cut a piece of tartan 51cm (20in) square and a piece of wadding 38.5cm (15in) by 51cm (20in).

Lay the tartan face down and lay the wadding on the top of the left side of the tartan. Now fold the remaining right side of the tartan over the wadding and tack it into place.

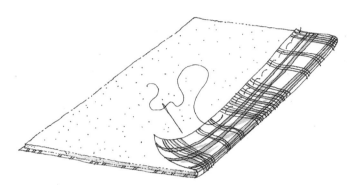

Cut a piece of plain red cotton 51cm (20in) by 25.5cm (10in) and lay it face up on the still exposed piece of wadding. Fold the tartan and wadding along the tacked seam in the same direction as before and tack into place.

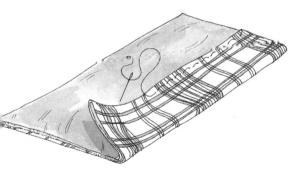

Using matching red cotton thread and leaving 2.5cm (1in) at each side, machine sew seams 2cm (¾in) apart across the tartan material, like this:

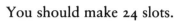

You should make 24 slots.

Now remove both rows of tacking stitches. If you've used white cotton for tacking it will be very easy to unpick them.

Round the still raw edges fold the tartan up over the wadding and red material and make a neat hem. You'll have to cut away a strip of wadding and red cotton to make this possible. Sew into place by hand.

Finally, make a narrow ribbon 89cm (35in) long from your tartan material. Fold in half and sew the fold in place like this:

Slide in your 24 coloured pencils and your present is ready to give, already wrapped. I would love to receive a present like this any time.

Daisy Chain Rocking Chair

The most ordinary or plain articles can be transformed with just a little paint. Tiny tins of enamel paint cost very little and can be found in most craft or DIY shops. As for your painting, it doesn't really matter how good you are at drawing. Sometimes the more naive it looks the better.

I once saw a children's playroom where the skirting boards were painted with simple animals, all types of animals going all the way round the room. Anyone could have done it but it looked marvellous. In another house the wall in a bathroom was painted with green reeds from floor to sink level. Higher on the wall was a set of china ducks. It really looked as if the ducks were flying from the reeds.

In the house where we photographed some of the children's presents, a cupboard had been painted, as an anniversary present, with a replica of the outside of the house. I can think of no present more personal than that.

Later on I will show how to stencil on plain wood but in the meantime I have painted this little rocking chair to show how good a little paint looks on any surface.

The chair was sanded with a fine sandpaper and then wiped with white spirit to remove any fine dust. I painted it with Dulux vinyl silk emulsion, two coats of pastel green, then when it was dry marked out the daisy chain with a pencil. I did it freehand, but you could trace a picture or a pattern if you prefer. I used Humbrol enamel paint to paint them. As a final touch you might like to make this that little bit more personal by painting the child's name on it.

Extra Special

Presents

Stencilled Chest of Drawers

There has recently been a broad-based revival of earlier crafts like weaving, quilting and stencilling, and I welcome it. These are crafts that give a home individuality, a home-made feeling in the literal sense of the word.

Stencilling is one of the earliest forms of interior design and I must warn you that, like chocolate, it's addictive. Once you start you might never stop. It's such fun, instantly rewarding and quickly done. What more can you want from a craft?

Stencils can be bought ready made, like the duck stencil I used on this little chest of drawers, or you can make them yourself. If you haven't stencilled before it is best to start with a properly made set, which you can buy in an art shop or good stationer's.

The paint that you use is very important and should be mixed to a fairly thick, toothpaste-like consistency. I used acrylic paint and it was terrific. It's a quick-drying water-based paint, easy to clean up and available in a glorious range of colours. Most art supply shops should have it.

Stencil brushes vary in size and are cylindrical. The bristles are all cut the same length forming a circular flat surface of bristle tips.

The stencil must be secured with masking tape to the object being stencilled. This is most important because if it is not secure paint will creep under the edges.

Dip only the flat bottom of the brush bristles into the paint and wipe any excess off on to a paper towel. Holding the brush upright stipple the paint on to the openings in the stencil.

Stippling is the proper term for the rapid up-and-down motion of the brush on the stencil. It's like hammering the paint on.

It is better to use too little paint at the start than too much.

The duck pattern had two stencils. The first did the body of the duck. Once that was dry I used the second stencil on top to produce the beak, wings and feet. When it was all dry I did the green leaves in the same way.

Use warm soapy water to wash the

brushes and wipe your stencils clean with a damp cloth because you can use them again and again.

I really enjoyed this and with a little practice it suddenly becomes almost easy. My husband Bruce says that for days after I did it I did nothing but stare at floors, ceilings, walls and doors. He said he felt that even the dog wasn't safe! There really is no limit. Even clothes, curtains, bedcovers and lampshades can be stencilled with special fabric paints.

Braided Tartan Rug

Braided rugs are recorded in painting and writing in America as early as 1827. The braiding of rags into rugs began as patchwork did, out of necessity. The early settlers in America simply couldn't afford to waste anything and their worn out garments, bedding and household furnishings that were no longer strong enough to be reworked into more clothing were used to make patchwork quilts and rag rugs. Even the smallest pieces could be used and I'm sure that's where the saying 'Waste not want not' came from.

Rag rug carpeting was a practical and durable floor covering. The rugs gave much needed warmth on the cold and draughty floors of poorly heated houses. They were easily cleaned and reversible.

Most of us nowadays no longer have these earlier needs and look on patchwork and braiding as folk crafts. When I finished this tartan rug I thought how warm and inviting it would be on a stone floor, and how lucky I was to be able to make it out of three gorgeous tartans without scrimping or saving.

It becomes difficult to plait if your strips of fabric are longer than 150cm (60in).

I cut mine 6.5cm (2½in) wide and varied the length between 100cm (39in) and 150cm (60in) so that the joins of the next strips would be in different places. This avoids nasty bumps that would occur if all three joins were in one place. Join the strips by cutting and sewing them at an angle. Use a needle and a slightly thicker cotton thread.

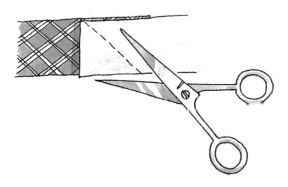

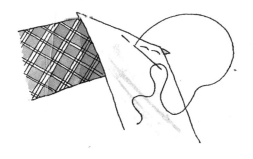

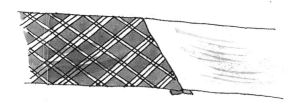

To start braiding, turn in the raw edges of your three strips like this:

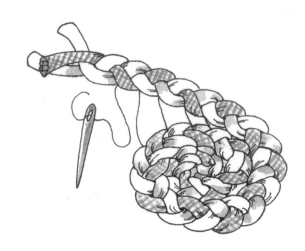

and pin them together.

Braid about three lengths of fabric together, sewing them on as you go. Then lay your plait on a flat and even surface and 'snail' the plait round and round. After you've done that start joining them together using a bodkin (a blunt needle) and a double strand of heavy button or carpet thread about a metre long. If it's longer it will tangle.

At no time should the bodkin pierce the fabric. You threat between the folds of fabric. This is what makes the rug reversible!

Whenever you join on a new lacing thread, tie it to the old one with a knot, the ends of which can be tucked back between the two loops of the plait.

You just keep plaiting and lacing until the rug is the size you want it to be. You must plait as evenly as possible and when you lace round corners be careful it's absolutely flat. If necessary, skip a loop on the plait you are joining to the body of the rug. It's not quite as simple as it seems but you should soon get the hang of it.

Lace Hankie Cloth

Surprisingly one of the most popular projects in my patchwork book was a tablecloth made out of twenty-five hankies. Since then I have been longing to make another hankie cloth using some of the Victorian lace hankies that I have collected over the years and now seemed an ideal time. It could make a perfect wedding present, a really extra special present for someone.

I started to sort through my hankies. Some needed mending, some needed washing, some were cream, a few were white but they were all gorgeous. I really enjoyed myself mending and washing, starching and ironing, and after a few days I had a pile of near-perfect hankies.

I sat down at our huge dining-room table and played with them for hours. As I moved them around like pieces of a jig-saw puzzle I could see enormous problems looming. For a start they varied in size from 12.5cm (5in) square to 30.5cm (12in) square. Most of them were plain in the middle with beautiful edges. The modern hankie cloth was made with hankies exactly the same size, fitting corner to corner with their rather boring plain edges covered with a length of broderie anglaise. With the antique hankies, however, this was not going to work. I hardly had three the same size let alone twenty-five, and the edges were the most beautiful part. It would be awful to hide them under a piece of broderie anglaise. I had to rethink my original idea.

As the children ate their meals in the kitchen I continued playing hankies on the dining-room table and it gradually dawned on me that they looked best overlapping each other, especially as some hankies were very thin. Overlapping also meant that it would still be possible to see the hankie that was underneath.

Much as I liked the transparent look of a lot of the hankies, it was obvious that I needed something to back them, something to sew them on to. I went back to John Lewis and bought 4 metres of butter muslin, the thinnest material I could find. It was 92cm (36in) wide. I cut it in half, joined it down the middle with a tiny running stitch to make it almost square and cut the selvage edge off because it was too dense and white (I could see it through the hankies). I folded the muslin in half and then in half again and found the centre, which I marked with a small safety pin (safety so it would not fall out).

I opened up the muslin, laid it on the table and started by laying a hankie in the middle. Then I worked out towards the edges. After laying about twelve hankies over and under each other, I began sewing from the middle using a tiny running stitch round the edge of each hankie. An old magazine under the muslin served to protect the table from my sewing.

Tamara came in while I was sewing these first hankies and her eyes widened. 'Do you know how many hankies you are going to need?' she asked. 'Hundreds!' she replied without waiting for my answer. I didn't actually need hundreds but I needed many more than I thought I would and ran out of them before I had finished. My entire family – mother, sister, husband, children – were all sent to every jumble sale and antique fair until I had enough. I loved every minute of it!

When it seemed that the nation's supply of old lace hankies had finally dried up I decided to finish the cloth off. Because of the way the hankies had fallen into place it seemed proper that the cloth should be round and I laid hankies round the outside edge with the points hanging down. I cut the butter muslin back to above the points of the hankies and stitched it to the hankies at the edges.

The diameter of my cloth is 176cm (68in).

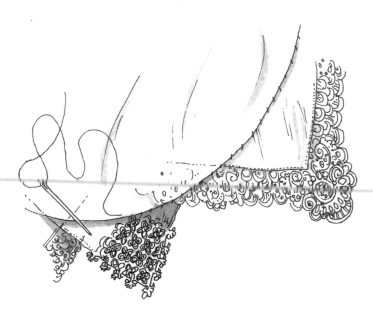

Of everything I've ever made I like this cloth the most.

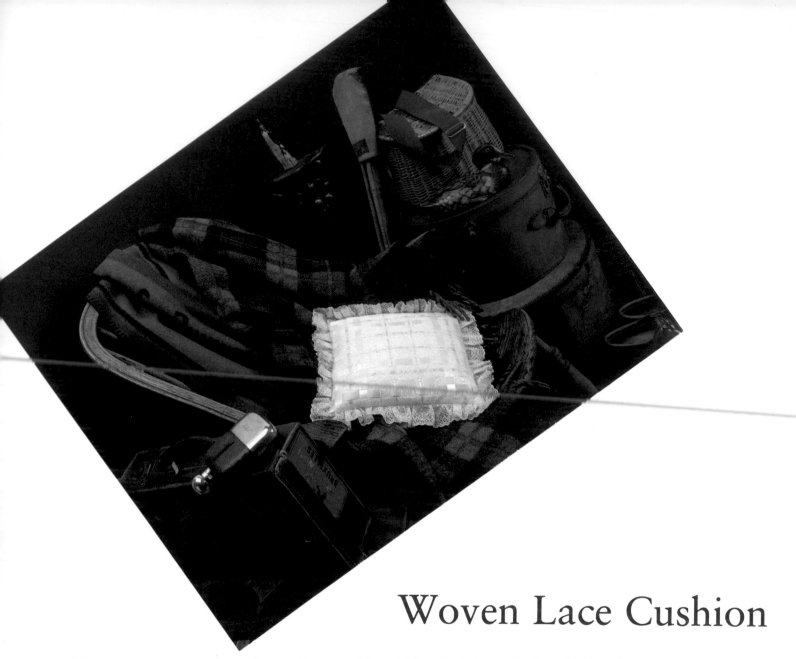

Woven Lace Cushion

Not everyone wants to hunt for weeks on end for old lace hankies and I thought that this present was a good idea for using pieces of new lace.

   This cushion is made from pieces you can buy in any haberdashery. To make a cushion that will be 30.5cm (12in) square you will need a piece of satin or cotton 33cm (13in) square for the back, 254cm (100in) of edging lace, a 15cm (6in) piece of cotton with snap fastenings, various pieces of ribbon and lace for the front and some ever useful fusable iron-on cotton.

   Cut all the pieces of lace and ribbon (but *not* the edging lace) into strips 33cm (13in) long.

   Cut a 33cm (13in) square of fusable cotton, lay it on the ironing board with the slightly shiny fusable side up and lay pieces of ribbon and lace side by side on it. Put a pin at an angle at the top of each piece.

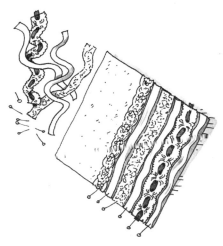

Take more of your pieces and weave them over and under the lace and ribbons you have already pinned and pin these new pieces at *both* ends.

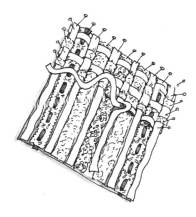

Straighten the first pieces you pinned by pulling them down and then pin them at the other end as well. Having made sure that everything is in place, cover with a thin cloth (to protect the lace and any ribbons which might be satin) and using a hot steam iron, iron outwards from the middle towards the pins. Remove the pins (from under the cloth) and iron out beyond the edges. This will fuse the lace and ribbon to the cotton. Now remove from the ironing board and machine stitch round the edge.

Gather up the edging lace until it fits round the edge. With the right side of the woven lace facing you pin the edging lace facing inwards.

Tack the edging lace in position by hand, removing the pins as you go.

Lay the square backing fabric on top of the woven lace front and the edging lace, right sides together, and tack into position by hand. Machine sew round leaving a gap of 15cm (6in) on one side.

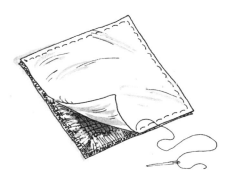

Remove the tacking stitches, turn right side out and, using ready-made strips of snap-on fasteners, sew a piece 15cm (6in) long on each side of the opening. It makes for easy washing. You need a 30cm (12in) square cushion to put in it.

Whenever I iron anything really important I use a piece of butter muslin. It's perfect for the job, thick enough to protect and thin enough to be able to see through.

Shells on Glass

Having collected so many shells for so long I have tried to think of interesting or attractive things to do with them, but the more I've tried the more obvious it has become that shells are best left just as they are. A glass jar or a basket full of shells is all right but gluing them on boxes or frames or making animals out of them makes even the most beautiful shells look unattractive.

One year, in Boca Grande on the west coast of Florida, I collected hundreds of the most vibrantly coloured tiny

*scallop shells I had ever seen. I have
returned to that beach many times since
but have never found them again. For
centuries, the scallop shell has been an
object of design in art, sculpture and
architecture. The Greeks imagined that
the goddess of love, Aphrodite, was born
from the scallop shell and every
Renaissance painter of any quality seemed
to adore the image. To most people
scallops are always Shell shells, oil
company shells.*

The first thing to do with any shells is to give
them a coating of polyurethane. Don't use
glossy. It looks too brash. Silk or matt finish
looks better and still brings up the colour
beautifully. They just look as if they are wet.

To make this present I had two pieces of
glass cut, 46cm (18in) by 36cm (14in).
After cleaning the glass with methylated
spirit I arranged the shells on one piece and
once they looked their best glued them on
with epoxy resin, using an orange stick as
applicator. *Use very little glue*, just on the
edges of the shells, and leave them to dry
overnight.

Strips of 1cm or ¼in wood are ideal for
gluing around the edges of the glass to prevent
the second piece of glass from crushing the
shells when it is put on.

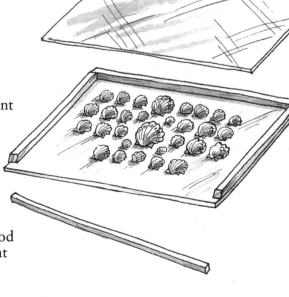

Before you frame the glass be sure to clean
all four sides of the glass thoroughly. Once
it is framed you won't be able to get at any
smudges on the inside! A rustic-looking wood
is lovely with shells although something that
looks like driftwood might be even better.

If this present is hung from a window it
looks as though the shells are suspended in
mid-air. They would look equally good with
a cardboard or fabric backing.

Yellow Flower Picture

Pressing flowers is something I have done since I was a child. I can remember pressing them in lots of different books hoping I'd forget some of them so I could have the surprise of finding them later. Oh, the pleasure of opening a book and finding faded rose petals or buttercups! I pressed some flowers from my wedding posy of wild flowers and made a little picture using a piece of silk cut from the inside pocket of my gorgeous Gina Fratini dress. Hopelessly sentimental, but there is something appealing about trying to capture a moment.

I've never really liked the smell of pot pourri but I've always loved the look of it. A large basket of crumpled flowers and petals looks scrumptious and has always intrigued me. How are the flowers made to look like that? The answer is that nothing special need be done. They can just be left to dry, but I also learned that flowers can be preserved by drying with desiccants.

There are several branded desiccants on the market and it's best to use one of them when dry-preserving flowers. Most of them contain silica gel which is the quickest desiccant you can use. Thin-petalled flowers like primroses can be dried in 24 hours. Put about 2.5cm (1in) of desiccant powder in a plastic box with a lid, something like a lunch or sandwich box, and lay your flowers face up on it. Gently filter more desiccant around and over the flowers (I used a kitchen strainer to do this) to cover them to a depth of 2.5cm (1in), put the lid on and keep in a warm place. All the moisture in the flowers will be absorbed by the powder. Don't overdry the flowers or they will become brittle.

About 24 hours later, or longer for heavier flowers, remove the lid and pour the powder off slowly, catching the flowers as they fall. They feel like paper and look lovely. Brush any excess powder off with a tiny paint-brush. The flowers can then be used as if they had been pressed. That's how I made this present.

Always use a rubber based glue like Copydex and an orange stick to stick them down. Choose your background colour carefully.

When it came to framing these yellow flowers I didn't want them squashed by the glass otherwise I would have used pressed flowers. The problem was solved by using two mounts. The extra thickness was enough to hold the glass off the preserved flowers. I made the frame from a do-it-yourself kit and painted it with enamel paint to match.

Daisies and Lace

When Tamara and I found these
pink-edged daisies last summer we thought
they were the biggest and most beautiful
we had ever seen and decided to press them.
Tamara has been pressing flowers since she
could stand and immediately went into
flower-pressing mode. She got out the
flower press and blotting paper, laid the
flowers face down on the paper, added
some leaves and stems in case we needed
them and covered it all with another piece
of blotting paper. She put the sandwich in
the press and tightened up the four screws. If
you don't have a flower press, blotting paper
in a large book will do.

We left these daisies for a month and you
should certainly never touch pressed flowers
for at least three weeks. A couple of months

would be better, in fact. Tamara thought they
looked gorgeous and asked me if I would do
something special with them. Well, when I
think special I think *lace* and in rummaging
through my bits and pieces came across this
little round dressing table mat.

The lace mat is backed with a piece of
pink paper and when I had finished putting
the daisies on it Tamara suggested that I add
some of the stems and leaves. I didn't agree
with her at the time but the more I look at
it now the more I tend to think she was
right.

The round frame came from a department
store and I simply painted it with enamel
paint to match the flowers.

Log Cabin Quilt

Over the years, the more American patchwork quilts I have seen the more I have found myself drawn to those made by the Amish people. Amish quilts are never made with patterned fabric. They are always plain, sometimes sombre, on occasion even severe. They are not gay or light but are basic and have a striking simplicity.

The Amish believe that their lifestyle must embody their faith in being a community to each other, devoted to God. They feel that individualism brings with it the demise of church, home and family.

The Amish people are Anabaptists. At the time of the Protestant Reformation, around 1525, one leader of an Anabaptist group that believed that one's primary allegiance must be to God rather than to the state was Menno Simons and his followers were eventually called Mennonites. In the late 1600s, a Mennonite minister, Jacob Amman, preached that the Mennonites had become lax in the discipline that separated Godliness from worldliness and he led a split from the Mennonites. His followers were later called Amish and their belief that involvement in the larger society of the world takes them away from family, community and the church still applies today.

The largest Amish community in America is in Pennsylvania and to look at them only superficially it would appear that they lead a drab, sombre existence, wearing plain dark clothes and black hats and denying themselves the 'conveniences' of modern life like automobiles or even indoor plumbing or electricity. But if you look closer there is a world of faith, community and beauty. This world looks after its members in precious, almost forgotten ways. It brings with it peace, security and contentment.

The most stunning patchwork quilts I have ever seen are those made by Amish women in the nineteenth century. These women never studied colour or line. Art for itself was and still is frowned upon within Amish communities. A quilt was to be functional, yet these women had such an instinctive eye for pattern and colour mix that there is nothing today that can match the almost mathematical beauty of some of these quilts.

A favourite pattern of quiltmakers in general in the nineteenth century was the log cabin and this design flourished amongst Amish quilters. Black fabric was often used on the 'dark' side of the log cabin block, almost as a counterpoint to the opposing plain but coloured material and when the blocks were sewn together yet another overall pattern was added to the finished quilt.

My log cabin quilt is made up out of 64 log cabin blocks. Each block is worked from a centre square outwards. Strips are added to one side at a time, rotating the square after each addition. All seams are straight and it does no harm to the finished patchwork if you stitch by machine. You'll need about 0.5 metre (20in) of material for the centres, and about 5 metres (5½ yards) each of dark and light material for the rest.

Cut all your fabrics into 4cm (1½in) wide pieces, and any length you like. I used four different greens, four different purples and pinks and put red squares in the middle. Traditionally the centre block is always red to signify the chimney. The strips of fabric round it signify the piled logs. I used four strips on each side and the finished block is 24cm (9½in) square.

Start with the centre square, which is 5cm (2in) square. Your first strip should be a light strip. Put the right sides together and sew a 1cm (⅓in) seam down one side.

Cut the strip off even with the centre square and open the first strip out.

Now lay the second light strip across the first strip and the square, right sides together, and stitch a 1cm (⅓in) seam. Again, cut the strip even with the square and open it out.

The third strip is your first dark strip. Proceed in the same way around the centre square. Always rotate in the same direction and keep adding strips until you reach the desired size block.

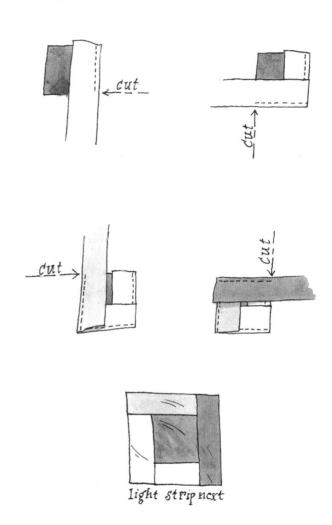

light strip next

Before you join your blocks together experiment with them. You'll be amazed at the variation you can achieve.

As the combination of vibrant colours and satin fabric proved almost overpowering, I decided that the quilt didn't need a border. Sheeting makes an excellent lining. It doesn't slip off the bed and is wide enough not to have a join in it. I chose a green sheeting and used medium weight wadding. Butt the edges of the wadding together and tack across.

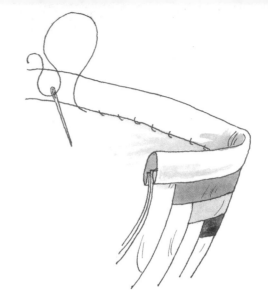

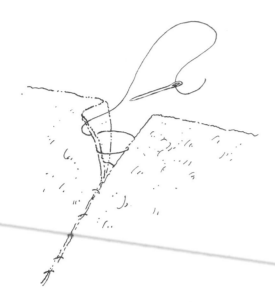

Lay your log cabin top face down on a flat surface (I like using the floor) and lay the wadding on top. Place the lining face up and tack all three layers together round the edges.

Cut 8cm (3in) wide strips of one of the fabrics you have used in the log cabin blocks, and join them together until you have enough to go round your quilt. Bind the edges.

Log cabin patchworks are one of the exceptions to the rule of elaborate quilting on patchwork. This might have been because the narrow width of the log strips created the problem of having to quilt through seam allowances all the time. However hard you might try, the quilting will not be fine. Most old log cabin patchworks were 'tied' or 'knotted' and that's what I did to mine.

Using a matching embroidery floss, take a large stitch at the corner of each block and tie it at the back. Leave the tufts of embroidery floss about 2.5cm (1in) long at the back.

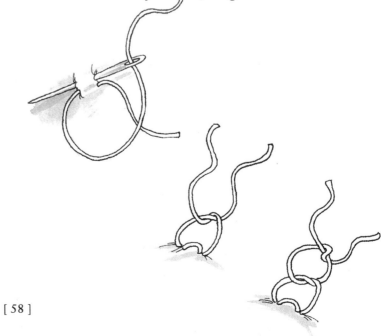

Christmas Presents

My mother's birthday is 16th December and she often receives what I call Christmas birthday presents. These are not presents to give at Christmas but presents that can be used at Christmas but given during the weeks before.

Nine days before Christmas my mind is firmly on course for the 25th. The children breaking up from school means carol concerts and nativity plays. The turkey and ham are ordered, the Christmas cake is ready to ice, most presents are bought or made, family has been invited and menus prepared. It's an impossible time to think of birthdays.

At the beginning of December, professional work permitting, I start making things for Christmas. I'll make wreaths, table and candle decorations, presents to hang on the tree and sometimes even an advent calendar but you have to start thinking about that in November.

I might be quite organised but I'm not always quite as good at it as I would like to be, so by mid-December I'm saying to myself, 'I think I'll make my mother one of these.'

Fircone Decorations

I enjoy working with natural things — flowers, leaves, feathers and shells, for instance — so when it comes to Christmas decorations I am in my element. It seems wrong, almost sacrilegious to have manmade, artificial decorations in December. It seems doubly wrong when you consider what is available: holly and ivy, conkers and chestnuts, acorns and every kind of nut. Maybe Bruce is right and I am a reincarnated squirrel. If that is the case it is the squirrel in me that adores fir cones. I love them! Whenever I see them I collect them, giant ones from Florida and most recently really sappy ones from trees in front of San Mineato Church in Florence, Italy.

Simply piling them in a wicker basket makes a beautiful sight. Over the years I've made so many things with them I could write a whole book about them and it was difficult deciding which three to include.

There are a few simple rules to follow in making fir cone decorations. Always use clear gloss polyurethane to give them their shine, but whereas chestnuts look wonderful when they are painted perfectly, cones do not. They look better when only the easy bits are roughly coated.

Each cone must be individually wired round some lower petals with florist's wire. (They aren't petals, but you know what I mean.)

I don't know what I'd do without florist's wire. (Bruce's father is a florist and he can

The final 'rule' is that you must have something to stick the wired cones into. Most florists sell ready made wreath bases made out of wired moss or Oasis. I used a lump of Das modelling clay to make the Christmas cake arrangement, a terrible waste of clay but it certainly helped me get that shape.

Other than this there are no rules. You can wire almost anything, acorn cups, beech nut cases, holly berries and small dried flowers. If you're handy with a drill you can wire hard things like chestnuts and walnuts or even nutmegs simply by drilling a hole for the wire. Drilled nutmeg smells out of this world. When you have finished what you are making and have a few spaces to fill in, use Uhu glue to stick acorns or hazelnuts in them.

repair *anything* with florist's wire!) It is available in rolls and is easily cut with wire cutters, or you can buy it in precut bundles. Once the wire is wrapped about the cone, twist the ends of the wire together and it's ready for use. Remember that the bottoms of cones are attractive, too. It's a good idea to show as many as possible.

Cone decorations can be made to hang on your door, surround candles or be a table centrepiece. Laying holly or ivy around cone table decorations looks terrific.

Holly Headbands

Having children to share Christmas with increased my already considerable enjoyment of the season enormously. For a start it meant that I didn't have to find an excuse to do the silly Christmassy things I enjoyed doing when I was younger, like dressing up. I like the idea of everyone dressing up for Christmas – me as well – and one Christmas I made everyone coloured felt headbands to

wear. They were a great success: too great, really, because everyone took theirs home. Since then I've made Father Christmas headbands, angel ones, ivy ones, mistletoe ones and holly ones, all of felt. Along the way tiny bells got added. These jingle when you move and when the children were younger and all came charging down the stairs together it really sounded as if Father Christmas and his reindeer had arrived.

To make each of these holly headbands I used scraps of three different colours of green felt, fourteen tiny red wooden beads, one metre (39in) of red ribbon and six tiny bells.

Cut a piece of dark felt 46cm (18in) long and 4cm (1½in) wide, fold it twice so that it's 1.5cm (½in) wide and stitch it down its length with a matching cotton.

Cut out about 26 holly leaves from the three different coloured felts and, using the red beads as berries, stitch the berries and leaves as you wish. Sew the bells on the bottom edge of the band about every 7.5cm (3in) and sew a red ribbon on each end.

Christmas Fairy

I could never find a really beautiful Christmas tree fairy, so in the end, as so often happens, I decided to make one. I had just finished making ours when a friend, a parent at Tamara's school, came visiting. Before I really knew what was happening I had agreed to make ten of these fairies to sell at the school Christmas charity bazaar. Making one Christmas fairy is fun. Making ten is another story! By the time I had finished I was sick to death of fairies and so I was very pleased that they were such a success at school. I could have sold them ten times over and people still ask me to make one for them.

You need two wooden macramé beads, one round and one elongated.

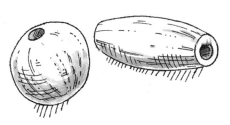

Paint the round bead a very pale pink. Glue the long bead on to one end of the round bead. Fold a pipe cleaner in half and twist it round the middle to make the arms.

Cut a strip of very thin wadding and wrap it round the arms and the body.

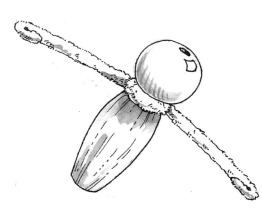

Stitch the wadding into place at the hands. You can glue the rest.
   Now make the wings and wand.
   Use milliner's wire and pieces of cut out

lace. Bend the wire into wing shapes, lay the lace on top and stitch it to the edges. Milliner's wire is very easy to use. You can make the wing shapes by bending the wire into a figure of eight, leaving a long end to wrap tightly twice round the middle of the body.

To make the wand I cut out a flower shape from some lace edging and stuck a pearl in the middle. I wound silver ribbon round a 10cm (4in) piece of wire and tied a bow at the bottom. Sew this to the pipe cleaner where the hand is supposed to be and stick the flower shape on the top.

Now for the dress.

I used a nylon lace with silver bits threaded through and some plain white wedding net for the petticoat. For the bodice cut a small piece of lace, wrap it round the body and glue it under the wings. Do the same with the sleeves, stitching the edges where the hands should be. I tied silver ribbon round the neck, fastened a bow at the back and stuck a piece of silver edging on the front of the bodice.

net the same size, put them all together and with a double thread gather up the top edge of all three pieces until it just fits round the bodice. Stitch it into place. I glued the seams at the back. Tie a silver ribbon round the waist and tie in a bow.

Silver lurex thread, sold for tying up presents, makes magnificent fairy hair. I put glue in a circle round the hole at the top of the head and laid pieces of thread 10cm (4in) long all the way round. When it was dry I cut the front pieces into a fringe. The crown was made with a piece of silver edging and I stitched a star-shaped sequin on the front. The eyes were painted with black enamel and the lips with red.

Take a piece of white tape 61cm (24in) long. Fold it in half and stitch it to the wadding and lace at the bottom of the bodice. This is to tie the fairy to the top of the tree.

Cut a piece of lace 117cm (46in) long and 21.5cm (8½in) wide. I stuck a silver edging along the bottom edge. Cut two pieces of

Pom Pom Bathmat

Quite by serendipity I was told how to make pom poms quickly and easily. I was in a wool shop in Horsham, Sussex,

explaining to the assistant that I wasn't sure how much wool I needed because I didn't know how many pom poms I could make out of one ball, when a voice said, 'Are you making lots? I hope you are not going to thread all that wool

*round a card.' I didn't know there was
any other way and turned around to ask
the owner of the voice, a tiny twinkly lady,
if she was privy to some dark pom pom
secret. She gave me the idea that I am
now passing on to you and when I said,
'Thank you,' she said, 'Don't thank me,
thank* Blue Peter. *I saw it on* Blue Peter.'
I hope I still watch Blue Peter *when I'm
her age. Here, then, is the easy way to
make pom poms.*

You will need a piece of wood about 23cm
(9in) long and 2cm (¾in) thick, and two
15cm (6in) nails. Hammer the nails right
through the wood about 7.5cm (3in) apart.

Wind the wool round and round the nails. I
used Pingouin Iceberg wool, which is machine
washable (that's important), and made four
pom poms out of each 50g ball of wool.

Once a quarter of a ball is wrapped round
the nails, slide it up the nails a little and tie a
piece of wool round the middle as tightly as
possible, leaving long ends to the tie.

As you slide one end off the nail, slip the
blade of a scissors in where the nail was
and cut. Do the same at the other end, shake
it all up and you have a pom pom ready for
trimming into shape. Ninety of these will be
enough to make a bath mat.

To make the backing for the mat, cut a
piece of hessian 48cm (19in) by 66cm
(26in) and iron on a piece of fusable iron-on
cotton the same size. Make a hem by
turning the hessian side up over the cotton
side. Secure the pom poms to the cotton
side by the long ends, using a large tapestry
needle. I put them in rows of ten.

Alex's Pot Pourri Bags

*It was Christmas week. The phone rang.
It was my sister.*

*'Where the hell's the pattern for the
pot pourri bags?'*

'What do you mean?'

*'In the patchwork book! Where are
the instructions?'*

'Instructions for what?'

'The pot pourri bags.'

'There aren't any.'

*'Yes there are, hanging on the wicker
chair.'*

*'You're supposed to make the
patchwork for the chair. The pot pourri
bags are just for decoration.'*

'Well that's silly.'

*She was right, but it was Christmas
week and I was preoccupied with other
things and the conversation left my mind
as soon as the receiver hit the phone.*

*Christmas Day arrived and with each
present my sister gave there were these
gorgeous pot pourri bags. Everyone
oohhed and aahhed over them and told
her how clever she was and so did I. It
made all her presents very special and
personal. At the end of the day as I kissed
my sister good-bye she hissed in my ear,
'You can have the pattern if you like.'
So, true to her word, here it is.*

You'll need:

Some pot pourri
0.5m (20in) each of Christmas pattern
fabric, plain red fabric and plain white fabric
– this is enough to make three bags
Rubber bands
Narrow red, green and white ribbons

Cut 25.5cm (10in) diameter circles out of
the plain and patterned fabrics. Alex says she
used a plate and just drew around it.

Place a plain circle and a patterned one
right sides together and machine sew a
narrow seam round the outside edge leaving
a gap of about 5cm (2in) or just enough to be
able to turn it right side out. Iron it flat,
turning the material at the gap under and
stitch this in place with a tiny hemming
stitch.

Lay about two large tablespoons of pot
pourri in the middle of the plain side.
Gather the circle up over the pot pourri and
secure it using a rubber band. Finally, tie two
narrow ribbons over the rubber band and
fasten them in a bow. They look lovely.

Father Christmas Mobile

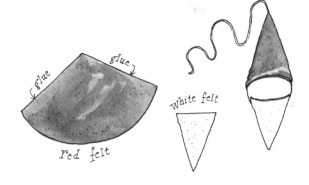

You'll need:

Red wool
Green wool
Tiny pieces of red and white felt
Red pipe cleaner
Red button thread
Red and black enamel paint
6 pieces of 0.5 cm (¼in) square modelling
wood, each piece 20cm (8in) long (model
shops sell it)
6 small wooden beads
A curtain ring

First I'll show you how to make a Father
Christmas. You can make all six at the
same time.

The beads will be the Father Christmases'
heads. Cut out a beard from the white felt
and a hat from the red felt so that they fit
the size of your bead, and glue them on with
Uhu glue. Make sure that the top hole of the
head is under the hat and the bottom hole
where the neck should be. Also make sure
that as you fold and glue the hat, you glue a
piece of red thread 20cm (8in) long to come
out of the top.

Take the green wool, fold it backwards and
forwards until there are about twelve strands
6.5cm (2½in) long and tie each end with a
small piece of red wool, like this:

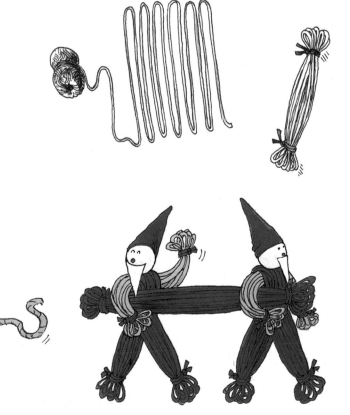

Do the same with the red wool but make the twelve strands longer, 11.5 cm (4½in) each and tie each end with a small piece of red wool.

Fold the middle of the red piece of wool over the middle of the green piece, wind red wool round the middle and tie it. The green piece makes Father Christmas's arms, the red piece his body and legs.

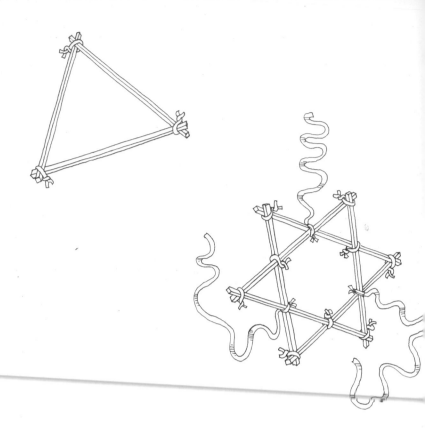

Tie three narrow red ribbons 20cm (8in) long to the wood and tie the other ends to a curtain ring ready for hanging. To finish, tie a Father Christmas to each of the outside points, using the thread coming out of his hat.

Glue Father Christmas's head to his wool body and paint three dots, two black ones for eyes and one red one for his nose. (His mouth is hidden by his beard.) I adore these Father Christmases and shall use them on hair bands next Christmas.

To make the support from which the Father Christmases will hang, lay out three pieces of the modelling wood to make a triangle and tie them together with red pipe cleaner. Just twist the pipe cleaner twice. Make another triangle with the remaining wood, lay them 'upside down' on top of each other and tie the two together.

Plaited Christmas Wreath

I used three different cotton fabrics with Christmas designs, and a bag of wadding, the kind you fill soft toys with.

Cut a strip from each fabric 140cm (56in) long and 16cm (6½in) wide. Fold the right sides together lengthways and machine sew a 1cm (½in) seam, then turn it right side out. I always do this using a large safety pin in one end, pulled through to the other. Once this is done stuff the tube with wadding.

This is easier said than done. The blunt end of a knitting needle and a great deal of patience were needed. Someone is bound to come along and tell me there is an easier way but I couldn't think of any when I was doing it.

Pin the three filled fabric tubes together and plait them. When you come to the end turn them into a circle. At this point unpin the other end and hand sew each piece to its matching other end. To do this evenly you will need to adjust the lengths of one or more of your pieces.

I used the red fabric with the Christmas trees to make a 13cm (5in) wide ribbon which I tied into a large bow and stitched over the joins in the plait. The small loop of red ribbon at the top of the wreath on the back makes it easy to hang.

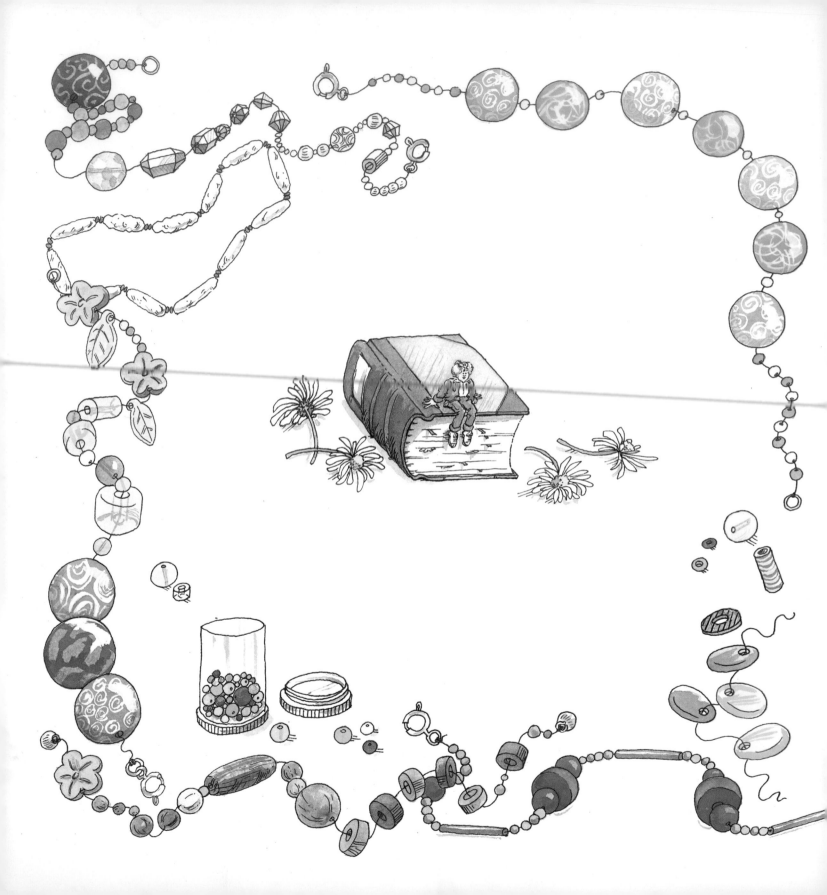

LAST MINUTE PRESENTS

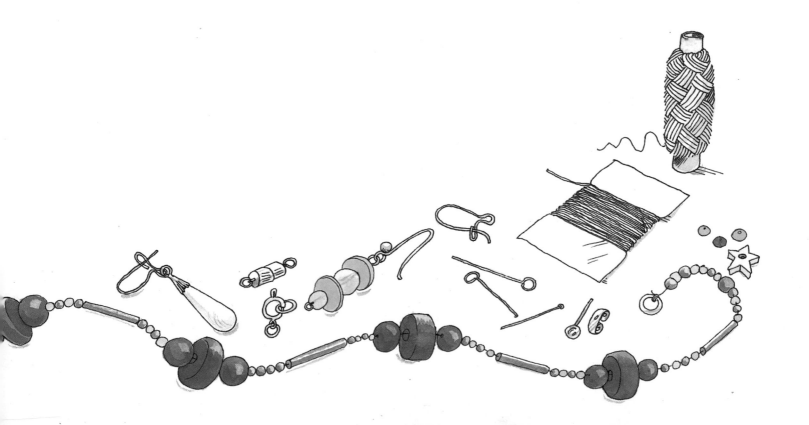

Lace Lampshade

This lace shade reminds me of mud, Wellington boots and Paris. Bruce and I were visiting an antique fair set up in a field on a large island in the Seine, on the outskirts of Paris. There were terrible storms with thunder and lightning and a great deal of rain. It poured and poured for days and days and the site got muddier and muddier. We squelched about in raincoats and Wellies and I bought a sodden pile of slightly muddy lace that I am sure the man was glad to be rid of. Oh, the pleasure of buying something for less than it ought to be!

All you have to do is measure the lampshade you want to cover from the bottom edge of one side, up and across the top and down to the bottom of the other side. Mine happened to be 56cm (22in).

Cut a circle of lace (neither damp nor muddy) with the same diameter as your lampshade.

Put a pretty edge round it and stitch it in place either by hand or by machine. Then just lay the lace circle over the shade and the bottom edge will hang just below the shade and look very pretty. They look lovely on lamps on both sides of the bed.

Oh yes, I nearly forgot. *Most important.* This shade is only decorative and you must use a low wattage light bulb. Otherwise you might singe it.

Pleated Paper Lampshade

You will need:
  1 sheet of marbled paper
  1 metre (39in) very thin ribbon
  A paper punch
  and no time at all!

Take a sheet of marbled wrapping paper and cut it into pieces 23cm (19in) wide (or the depth of the lampshade you want to cover).

Join the pieces together using a good paper glue like Copydex until you have one piece measuring 330cm (130in) by 23cm (9in).

Using a pencil and ruler, make a line every 2cm (¾in) and using them as your guide fold the paper up like a concertina.

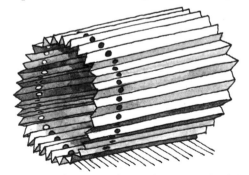

Join the two ends with glue and using a hole puncher make a hole 2.5cm (1in) from the top in each fold. Thread a very thin matching ribbon through the holes, tie in a bow and slip the pleated shade on top of your lampshade.

You can, if you wish, make several of these. I made three out of children's wrapping papers and gave them to a little girl who was going to have to be in bed for quite a while. She could change them each evening. Tigers and lions going round one evening and coloured flowers the next. I enjoyed that.

Wine Bottle Cover

Bruce and I usually go off clutching bottles of wine when we have dinner at friends' houses. For one birthday dinner I wanted to make the bottle look a little more like a present and made this bottle cover in half an hour. Honest. For an average size wine bottle you need a piece of material 28cm (11in) by 36cm (14in) and a piece of thin ribbon 76cm (30in) long.

Put the selvage along one of the 28cm (11in) sides and fold the right sides together. Fold your ribbon in half and place the fold in the seam 7.5cm (3in) from the selvage edge and stitch a seam down the side.

Turn it right side out. Turn a 1.5cm (½in) hem at the bottom and using double thread stitch right round, gather it all up as tightly as possible and finish off by knotting the thread carefully.

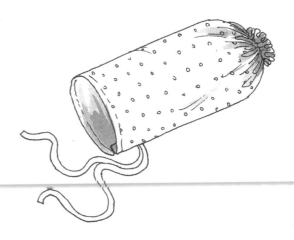

This little gathered bit fits into the hole in the bottom of the wine bottle. (It's not a hole but you know what I mean.) I'm told you can knit wine bottle covers, but I bet you can't do it in half an hour!

Hankie Sachets

Strange things thrill me. I love hearing stories of wedding dresses turned into lamp shades, of ball gowns turned into dungarees, of broken china turned into mosaic picture frames, even of warehouses turned into townhouses. I enjoy hearing these stories because I am attracted to the concept of recycling.

Turning face flannels into dog towels and hankies into tablecloths were satisfying patchwork ideas and here are two more quick and simple ideas for turning something ordinary into something that's a bit different.

For the first I used a large, plain man's hankie with the initial 'E' (to give to my daughter Emily). Spotted or paisley hankies, table napkins, tray cloths or anything else that is square would also do.

Iron the hankie flat and turn three corners into the middle, like an envelope. Hand sew the edges of these folds together, from the centre outwards using tiny stitches. Then sew a button in the middle where the corners meet and make a loop on the top of the other corner.

Kleenex reigns today and Emily doesn't use hankies. She'll probably use this little bag for her jewellery.

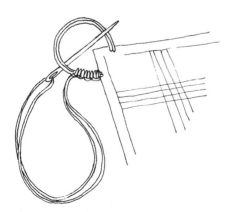

I can remember my grandmother having what she called a runner on her sideboard in the hall: a long narrow piece of embroidered linen to protect the surface of the wood.

My grandmother was not alone and my sister Alex has collected runners for years. Whenever I see one at a jumble sale or flea market I buy it for her. I used one to make this little sachet.

This runner is 77cm (30in) long. I folded 25.5cm (10in) of it back on itself, pinned it and sewed the sides together using a blanket stitch which continued round the part of the runner that would be the flap. That's all there is to it. A simple present finished in half an hour. The same idea works well with a piece of cotton or linen. Just turn an edge in and blanket stitch all the way round. Adding an initial or a date always adds a personal dimension and enhances the pleasure of receiving the gift.

This one is made out of plastic and raffia and to make it you just need three circles of plastic, some raffia and a hole puncher. My circles are dinner plate size, 27cm (10½in) in diameter. Two circles are used for the back and the third, folded in half, for the front. Use double-sided Sellotape to keep your circles in place and punch holes at even intervals all the way round. Once you have done that and removed the tape (this is important – it shows through the plastic), lace round the edge using your raffia.

The holder can be suspended by a small loop glued to its back. A round or triangular shaped ring can be used but I wish I had thought of making a raffia loop for it.

Kitchen Napkin Holder

When one of my children was at nursery school (it's awful but I can't remember which one!) she (or he) proudly brought home a holder just like this one, made out of two cardboard picnic plates. I used it in the kitchen until it finally fell apart.

Bath Mitten

You will need:

Small piece of Liberty print (about 38cm/15in square)

Small piece of towelling (you could use a face flannel)

23cm (9in) piece of narrow elastic

Cut a piece of flannel 15cm (6in) by 28cm (11in) with one of the finished edges along the shorter side.

Fold a piece of Liberty fabric in half and cut out a double piece the same size as the flannel you have already cut. Place them on top of each other right sides together with the fold in the fabric and the finished edge of the flannel together. Draw the shape of your mitten at one end and then sew round this line with your sewing machine.

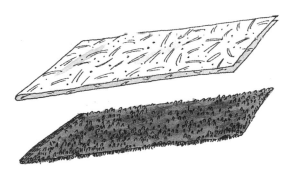

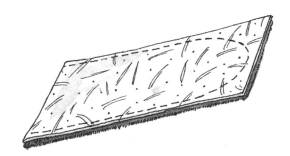

Now cut away the surplus fabric from the mitten shape.

The seam needs to be oversewn: do this using a small zig-zag all the way around. If you are actually making this bath mitten as you read I hardly need tell you why for by now you'll be covered in bits of towelling. It's dreadful stuff! After you have finished oversewing the seam turn the mitten inside out.

Cut a strip of Liberty print 31cm (12in) long and 5cm (2in) wide. Turn each side of it in and iron it and you will have a strip that is 2.5cm (1in) wide. This will be sewn around the wrist of the mitten for the elastic to go through.

Using your sewing machine, stitch one side of this ribbon on to your mitten 4cm (1½in) from the open end and then stitch the other side nearer the open end to form a tunnel through which you should thread the elastic. Draw the elastic slightly, to the tension you require, and then stitch into place.

I put a little loop on the side so that I could hang the mitten up. When I made this mitten I made three at the same time and it took me an evening. You should be able to make one in an hour.

Cards

I like popping surprises into cards. A few stickers, a needle case, a hairband, a hankie or a scarf.

Hankies are perfect in cards – lace ones, Liberty ones or even a plain man's one. I like men's hankies almost as much as the pretty ones. I'm thinking of making a summer skirt out of those lovely blue stripy ones!

Over the years, Emily, Ben, Tamara and I have made every kind of card you can imagine. We've made them with pressed wild flowers, leaves and ferns. We have pencilled, painted and stencilled, cut bits out and stuck bits on. Ben's cards have always been the most inventive and comical and his drawing ability is way beyond mine. His most recent card for my sister, with large smiling teeth that turned out to be the 'H' of 'Happy Birthday' when it was opened, made everyone laugh.

Here are two of my simplest and most used ideas.

Using multicoloured paper from an art supply shop, fold a piece in half to serve as your card. Cut out a shape with an artist's scalpel or small Stanley knife – I've used hearts and butterflies, but you could vary this by using letters, numbers, other animals, anything you like. Fold a hankie and put it in the card, holding it in place with two pieces of double-sided Sellotape. I used a fine gold felt tip pen to outline the cut-out shapes. You could also add Happy Birthday or Thank You or simply a name.

Cards with post cards are really my favourites. Any post card will do, although genuine old ones are delightful. Just stick the postcard on a folded piece of coloured paper and you have a delightful and original card.

Making an envelope for your card is simple. Take a square of paper large enough to take your card and fold three corners into the middle overlapping them just enough to glue them together.

Necklaces and Bracelets

At the Bead Shop in Covent Garden you can buy everything you need to make really professional jewellery. You will find every kind of bead imaginable, but most important of all they sell the *findings*.

Findings are the metal pieces you use to finish your jewellery: things like earring wires and hooks, head pins, jump and bolt rings, screw clasps, box clasps, calottes and spacer bars. They also sell a variety of threads. The Bead Shop mail order catalogue is so beautiful with pictures of hundreds of coloured beads that it is worth sending for just for itself. Their address is 43 Neal Street, London WC2.

Tamara and I got very enthusiastic recently about magatama beads. These have off-centred holes, and when threaded fold into each other in a most attractive way. We used them for the short blue and clear necklaces at the top of the photo. I use either waxed terylene or nylon for threading on and when we have put the clasps on I dab the knot with colourless nail polish. Better safe than sorry.

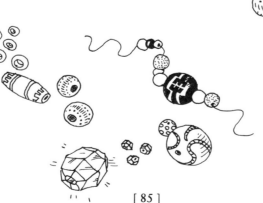

[85]

Shell Cocktail Sticks

I was pleased with this idea for using up some of my shells.

I painted each shell with a coat of polyurethane. To do this I perched them on blobs of BluTack and coated one side. After they dried I turned them over and coated the other sides. When they were ready they were stuck on to wooden cocktail sticks using epoxy resin glue.

I got quite carried away, soon had a production line and ended up with hundreds of these cocktail sticks. They make lovely presents just tied with ribbon into bundles or put in small cardboard boxes.

Wrapping Presents

The Art of Gentle Concealment

The idea that anything, no matter how cheap or expensive or large or small, can be beautiful finds one of its greatest outlets in gift wrapping.

The concept of improving the beauty of an object through its wrapping is most profound in Japanese culture and is central to their traditional sense of beauty. Gardens are 'wrapped' by various fences, food is 'wrapped' in lacquer containers and presents, even the most humble, are wrapped with simple elegance.

In Japan gift giving is still a highly ritualised custom. Japanese culture dislikes the blunt and the direct, preferring the indirect and restrained and these rules apply both to the giving of gifts and to the wrapping of them. It would be discourteous in Japanese eyes to give an unwrapped gift. It would be crude and vulgar. This restraint means that in Japan the wrapping of presents has literally become an elegant and refined art form.

The Japanese concept that something should be beautifully concealed, no matter how troublesome or inefficient the act may be, so that whoever receives it will actively enjoy opening the present, is an idea that I adore. A wrapping should of course protect the present you are giving, but the paper you use, the colour, the ribbon and the way it is tied, all these things should reflect the way you

feel about the person you are giving the present to. In Japan it is said that giving a gift is like wrapping one's heart. Here, too, we should consider the wrapping and giving of presents as a token of love and consideration.

Wrapping Bottles

In Japan it is traditional to use a square piece of fabric to wrap awkward objects. It is called a 'furoshiki'.

The corners are drawn up and knotted into a makeshift handle. The softness of cloth, as opposed to the stiffness of paper, opens up all sorts of aesthetic possibilities.

Here is how to wrap one bottle with a square of fabric.

Here are two ideas for wrapping two bottles.

Either:

Or:

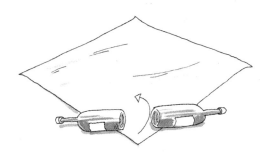 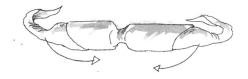

Wrapping Jars of Homemade Jam

Here are two ideas for making jam jars look more interesting. Material such as gingham looks lovely but paper will do just as well. If you do use material be sure to pink the edges with pinking shears.

Wrapping Several Small Objects

If you want to give someone golf or tennis balls this would be perfect. Tissue paper is ideal for this sort of wrapping. I once saw children's gob stoppers (what a dreadful name) wrapped like this. Any sweets would look enchanting.

Wrapping a Rounded Object

Rounded objects are difficult to wrap but pleating the paper round overcomes many of the problems. This wrapping would look great on a cake.

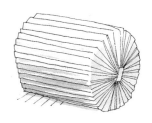

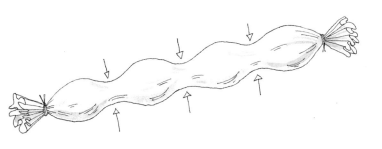

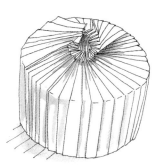

You can add a little something on the top if you like; a bell or a fircone, for instance.

Wrapping a Plant, a Flower or a Posy

A plant is a lovely gift whether it's wrapped or not, but I was enchanted with this traditional Japanese way of wrapping a plant in red and white washi. (That's hand made Japanese paper.)

You need two squares of paper, the red one a little smaller than the white.

Wrap a ribbon around the plant and tie at the front. You can wrap a single flower or a posy in the same way.

Although I have shown you how to wrap some awkwardly shaped presents, my advice is that it's always best to put unusual shaped gifts into boxes or tins – old biscuit tins or shoe boxes, for example. If your present is too small for your box, shred some tissue paper by cutting it into thin strips and stuff it all around the gift before putting the lid on. To make your presents really neat, make the most of double-sided Sellotape. Use it to seal things so that the sealing doesn't show. I like to wrap my presents up in layers because I love watching people opening their gifts. There should be at least three layers, tissue paper around the present itself, the box and finally the wrapping around the box. If you want to extend your pleasure double wrap your gift, although this little indulgence should be used sparingly.

You will see that I have used a wide variety of materials to wrap presents in. You really can use anything. Fabric always looks elegant. Scrunched aluminium foil wraps around awkward shapes. Cellophane can be used to wrap leaves or flowers or even one or two of those tiny Cadbury Neapolitan chocolates around presents, especially those

for children. If you use cellophane use some plain tissue paper first.

Doilies, especially the silver and gold ones, are very effective for wrapping. Simply wrap a present in any type of paper, then wrap one or two doilies around it and tie it with a ribbon. Plain brown paper can be surprisingly effective and it's easy to make it unusual. I once gave my son Ben a present wrapped in ordinary brown paper, tied together with string and smothered in old used stamps from Italy and France. You can just as easily add stickers or cut out pictures or small fir cones or jingly bells to your wrapping. And even if you are out of wrapping paper there is always something available, paper napkins or even paper towels. Wrapping just takes a little imagination and the presents that are illustrated here show a few of my ideas. By spending a little time thinking about the wrapping I have made the gifts more personal. It's easy for you to do the same. Just give your imagination free reign and you are bound to create marvellous and unique wrapping.